The UNITED STATES
in WORLD WAR II

1941–1945

★★ *The Drama of* **AMERICAN HISTORY** ★★

The UNITED STATES
in WORLD WAR II

1941–1945

Christopher Collier
James Lincoln Collier

Benchmark Books

MARSHALL CAVENDISH
NEW YORK

ACKNOWLEDGMENT: The authors wish to thank Tom Paterson, Professor Emeritus, University of Connecticut, for his careful reading of the text of this volume of The Drama of American History and his thoughtful and useful comments. The work has been much improved by Professor Paterson's notes. The authors are deeply in his debt, but, of course, assume full responsibility for the substance of the work, including any errors that may appear.

Photo research by James Lincoln Collier.

COVER PHOTO: *U. S. Army Center of Military History*

PICTURE CREDITS: The photographs in this book are used by permission and through the courtesy of: *Corbis*: 10, 11, 17, 20, 31, 53, 57, 64, 76, 84; *Library of Congress*: 26, 27; *National Archive*: 73, 77, 80; *New York Public Library*: 21, 22, 25, 34, 39, 41, 54, 62, 63, 67, 69; *U. S. Army Center of Military History*: 33, 37, 38, 42, 45, 47, 51, 55, 59, 71, 72, 86.

Benchmark Books
Marshall Cavendish Corporation
99 White Plains Road
Tarrytown, New York 10591-9001

Library of Congress Cataloging-in-Publication Data

Collier, Christopher, (date)
World War Two / by Christopher Collier and James Lincoln Collier.
p. cm. — (The drama of American history)
Includes bibliographical references and index.
ISBN 0-7614-1316-2
1. World War, 1939-1945—United States—Juvenile literature. 2. World War, 1939-1945—Juvenile literature. [1. World War, 1939-1945—United States. 2. World War, 1939-1945.]
I. Title: World War 2. II. Title: World War II. III. Collier, James Lincoln, (date) IV. Title.
D769 .C65 2001
940.53'73—dc21   00-051874

Printed in Italy

1 3 5 6 4 2

CONTENTS

PREFACE

Over many years of both teaching and writing for students at all levels, from grammar school to graduate school, it has been borne in on us that many, if not most, American history textbooks suffer from trying to include everything of any moment in the history of the nation. Students become lost in a swamp of factual information, and as a consequence lose track of how those facts fit together and why they are significant and relevant to the world today.

In this series, our effort has been to strip the vast amount of available detail down to a central core. Our aim is to draw in bold strokes, providing enough information, but no more than is necessary, to bring out the basic themes of the American story, and what they mean to us now. We believe that it is surely more important for students to grasp the underlying concepts and ideas that emerge from the movement of history, than to memorize an array of facts and figures.

The difference between this series and many standard texts lies in what has been left out. We are convinced that students will better remember the important themes if they are not buried under a heap of names, dates, and places.

In this sense, our primary goal is what might be called citizenship education. We think it is critically important for America as a nation and Americans as individuals to understand the origins and workings of the public institutions that are central to American society. We have asked ourselves again and again what is most important for citizens of our democracy to know so they can most effectively make the system work for them and the nation. For this reason, we have focused on political and institutional history, leaving social and cultural history less well developed.

This series is divided into volumes that move chronologically through the American story. Each is built around a single topic, such as the Pilgrims, the Constitutional Convention, or immigration. Each volume has been written so that it can stand alone, for students who wish to research a given topic. As a consequence, in many cases material from previous volumes is repeated, usually in abbreviated form, to set the topic in its historical context. That is to say, students of the Constitutional Convention must be given some idea of relations with England, and why the Revolution was fought, even though the material was covered in detail in a previous volume. Readers should find that each volume tells an entire story that can be read with or without reference to other volumes.

Despite our belief that it is of the first importance to outline sharply basic concepts and generalizations, we have not neglected the great dramas of American history. The stories that will hold the attention of students are here, and we believe they will help the concepts they illustrate to stick in their minds. We think, for example, that knowing of Abraham Baldwin's brave and dramatic decision to vote with the small states at the Constitutional Convention will bring alive the Connecticut Compromise, out of which grew the American Senate.

Each of these volumes has been read by esteemed specialists in its particular topic; we have benefited from their comments.

CHAPTER I

The Legacy of World War I

Wars do not just happen. They come about because of past events, and the way people react to current events. The causes of World War II are complex, and are still argued over by historians, but the general picture is clear enough.

It was truly a world war, fought in Asia, Africa, Europe, the Middle East, on land, on sea, and in the air. The death and destruction wrought makes World War I, which was horrible enough, look like small potatoes. Although solid figures are hard to come by, some 30 million people died in World War II. Billions of dollars worth of property, including whole cities like Dresden, Hiroshima, and Warsaw, were destroyed. Great empires vanished like morning fog in the sun. Hundreds of millions of people found their lives permanently transformed. One historian has called it "the largest single event in human history."

Yet it is becoming increasingly clear that it need not have happened. For some time after the war many people believed that World War II was simply a continuation of World War I, and was probably inevitable. However, historians now believe that the Germans under Adolf Hitler could have been stopped at the beginning. The failure of the democracies,

World War II left cities, towns, and villages like this town along the Rhine in ruins. Tens of millions were made homeless, perhaps as many as 30 million died from bombs, disease, and famine.

especially France, Great Britain, and the United States, to do so was a major cause of the war. In this chapter we shall see why this happened.

For several centuries before 1900, France was the dominant power on the European continent. After about 1870, Germany began to gain in economic and military power, until the French felt threatened. Over these years France and Germany each entered into defensive alliances with other nations, and when a conflict broke out between small Serbia and great Austria, other European nations were drawn in. By August 1914, Europe was at war. Germany and its allies nearly won, and would have except for the aid Americans gave to France, England, and their allies, first as supplies and loans of money, and, in 1917, with American troops.

These tipped the balance, and in November 1918, Germany surrendered. (For the story of the United States in World War I, see the volume in this series called *The United States Enters the World Stage*.)

World War I had seen the slaughter of tens of thousands of young men, who would rise from trenches to rush across ruined fields in the face of withering machine-gun fire and incessant shelling, to die painfully with arms and legs blown off, or hang screaming from barbed-wire fences trying to hold their intestines in until death mercifully came. Poison gas ripped at soldiers' lungs, leaving them to choke out short lives thereafter. Long before the war was over, soldiers were asking themselves what it was for.

In World War I soldiers would rise from their trenches to charge into no-man's-land with little hope of surviving. The slaughter sickened people and made them reluctant to get into war again. Here American troops are seen in trenches.

Given this feeling, at the peace conference at Versailles near Paris in 1919 the victors, especially France, were determined to punish the Germans, and harsh terms were imposed: The Germans were forbidden to raise a significant military force, shorn of territory and colonies, and were required to make enormous payments called reparations, to the victors. These terms left the Germans feeling bitter and angry toward the victors, and eager for revenge. Making matters worse, the heavy reparations payments helped to create immense financial difficulties for Germany, as the nation tried to recover from the war.

The United States got into World War I late—Americans in general felt that it was not their war until German submarines began sinking American ships. The nation did not suffer much during the war; indeed, it came out of the war more powerful than before. Nonetheless, tens of thousands of American men had fought in the trenches, nearly 50,000 killed in action, another 60,000 dead of disease, and about 230,000 wounded. Increasingly, Americans began asking themselves if the war had been worth it. Pacifism—the idea that war should be avoided at all costs—was on the rise.

Beyond this, there was in America a wish for "normalcy," and a turning inward: The nation, many believed, ought henceforward to stay out of the affairs of Europe, which seemed to them a tired, confused—indeed, immoral—continent.

Not all Americans agreed: In particular, President Woodrow Wilson wanted desperately for the United States to join the new League of Nations, which he himself had been instrumental in creating. But public opinion in America was against Wilson, and in the end the United States never joined the League, although it often cooperated with it for specific purposes.

In Europe there remained much despair and confusion. The economic situation in Germany was particularly bad. Burdened by the reparations, the nation suffered tremendous inflation. By 1923 a single

European National Borders,
1919–1935

Atlantic Ocean

FINLAND

NORWAY

SWEDEN

ESTONIA

LATVIA

LITHUANIA

North Sea

Baltic
Sea

DENMARK

RUSSIA

EAST
PRUSSIA
(Germany)

EIRE

ENGLAND

London

NETHERLANDS

•Berlin

•Warsaw

Brussels

GERMANY

POLAND

RHINELAND

•Paris

Prague

CZECHOSLOVAKIA

FRANCE

Vienna

Budapest

ROMANIA

SWITZERLAND

AUSTRIA

HUNGARY

Bucharest

YUGOSLAVIA

Black
Sea

Sarajevo

Belgrade

BULGARIA

ITALY

Sofia

PORTUGAL

CORSICA

•Rome

ALBANIA

GREECE

TURKEY

SPAIN

SARDINIA

Athens

SICILY

CRETE

SCALE of MILES

0   250   500

Mediterranean Sea

American dollar was worth *4 billion* German marks. Yet despite everything, Europe began to rebuild, and by the late 1920s the situation had
improved. Economic problems continued, especially in Germany through
the 1920s and 1930s, but Europeans were becoming more hopeful. A
number of conferences were held that resulted in agreements and treaties

Europe on the Eve of World War II:
German and Soviet Expansion
by September 1939

German Control

intended to prevent another awful war from happening. Among the most important of these was the naval reductions conference of 1922, by which Great Britain, Japan, and the United States agreed to limit the size of their fleets. The Locarno Conference in 1924 and the Kellogg-Briand Pact also were aimed at keeping the peace. In 1926 Germany was allowed to join the League of Nations.

Thus, by the end of the 1920s, between the various peace conferences and the easing of the financial situation, it appeared that Europe might pull itself out of the mess left by World War I. However, in the United States, the American stock market had risen to dizzying and, as it turned out, totally unrealistic heights. The nation seemed to be enjoying great prosperity, but, in fact, millions of Americans, especially farmers and laborers, were not sharing in the good times. In October 1929 the stock market collapsed and began a long slide downward. The United States spiraled into the worst economic depression in its history. The Depression spread to a still financially wobbly Europe. And now began the chain of events that led directly to World War II.

Wars are fought for many reasons—for territory, for power, for sources of raw materials like oil and iron ore, for the ambitions of rulers. World War II involved all of these things; but it was also about something equally important—ideas. The term we use for sets of related ideas is *ideology*. World War II, among other things, pitted the ideology of fascism against the ideology of democracy.

The fascist ideology varied from country to country where it took hold, but it had a common basis: strong, centralized government controls, virtually total and thus called totalitarian. Fascist governments promised to get things done quickly—usually without concern for individual rights—where democracies might wrangle for years over the best course to take. The fascists were also *militaristic*: They believed that war was natural to nations, and that the mighty had every right to rule their neighbors by force if they could. In addition, the German fascists believed that the "Teutonic" peoples, including Germans, Scandinavians, and the English, were a superior "race." Others, like Jews, Slavs, Asians, and Africans, were naturally inferior and by rights the Teutonic, or "Aryan," people ought to rule. Finally, fascists believed that "the State," that is, the nation, was more important than the individual. Private citizens should be prepared to sacrifice anything, including their lives, for the good of the state.

The fascist ideology was directly opposed to the democratic ideology, especially the American one, which said that "all men are created equal," and that individuals have certain basic rights, like freedom of speech and the right to participate in government, which governments cannot violate. Thus, while World War II was fought for many reasons, there was a strong feeling on the part of Americans and their allies that it was being fought to preserve democracy from the fascists.

Why would any people choose to live under a fascist government? In some cases, of course, they had no choice: The fascist dictators simply took over one way or another. But World War I had left many European nations in chaos, with high unemployment, raging inflation that left salaries and savings worth less every minute, with governments torn by several parties competing for power, with bribe taking and payoffs a way of life in government and business. Millions yearned for order and discipline, which was precisely what the fascists promised.

The first to take advantage of this desire for order was an Italian, Benito Mussolini. The son of a blacksmith, he began as a newspaper reporter, and was active in politics. After the chaos of World War I he adopted fascism. He formed groups of toughs who wore black shirts. These Blackshirts deliberately caused riots and disorder, which they then used as an excuse to bring in troops to put down. Italians began to believe that only Mussolini and his fascists could save Italy from collapse, and in 1922 Mussolini took over. He outlawed other parties, imprisoned his enemies, sometimes torturing them. However, to many people, both Italians and outsiders, it appeared that Mussolini had accomplished much that was good. He got industry going, drained malarial swamps, and as many noted, made "the trains run on time."

Meanwhile, a far more vicious fascist was making his way forward in Germany. Adolf Hitler has been seen as one of the archcriminals of all times, and it is hard to argue with this opinion. Born in Austria, a German-speaking nation, he initially hoped to be an artist. He served in the German army during World War I, and after the war joined a tiny German political party, the National Socialist German Workers' Party, generally known as the Nazis.

In 1923 the Nazis tried to seize control of the government of Bavaria,

Adolf Hitler was, even during the war, considered one of the archcriminals of humanity, but few realized how terrible his deeds actually were until the concentration camps were discovered.

a section of Germany. The attempt failed and Hitler was put in jail, where he wrote *Mein Kampf* (*My Struggle*). In this book he laid out for all to see his hatred of Jews, his insistence on the superiority of the "Aryans," his anticommunism, his plans for German domination. *Mein Kampf* seemed like the ravings of a madman, and few people took the book seriously. Hitler was released from jail after a year, and although the Nazis gained a little, by 1928 they held only 12 of 491 seats in the German legislature.

Then came the Depression. By 1932 German incomes were down 40 percent and 6 million people were out of work. The Nazi program, blaming Germany's problems on Jews, international businessmen, and the punitive peace of Versailles with its heavy reparations, appealed mightily to many Germans. Support for the Nazis increased dramatically. Hitler's anticommunism was particularly important because in 1917 the Communists had taken over Russia, and were hoping to start Communist revolutions elsewhere.

Under Communist theory all resources were meant to be shared: But in its Russian form nearly all businesses were run by the government. German businessmen saw that if communism came to their nation they would lose their wealth and power. Actually, the Communists were not much of a threat in Germany, but still German businessmen were willing to help Hitler as a wall against communism. The army was also very powerful in Germany at the moment, and in 1933, with the support of the army and big business, Hitler and the Nazis came to power. Very quickly, through devious means, Hitler eliminated other political parties, and gathered all power into his own hands.

He now began to secretly build up the German army, an action that was forbidden by the Versailles peace treaty. In the fall of 1933 he took Germany out of the League of Nations and in general began violating the terms of Versailles. Then, in March 1936, he sent troops into the Rhineland, a section of Germany bordering France that was supposed to be neutral ground. The British and the French protested but did nothing. Why?

This is the crucial point: In 1936 British, French, and American men who had seen the horrors of World War I were in their forties. Young people who had lost their fathers, uncles, or older brothers in the war were in their twenties. Widows still had pictures of dead husbands in their uniforms on their mantelpieces. World War I was fresh in peoples' minds, and as much as they feared fascism, the thought of getting into another war with Germany was even worse. So they turned a blind eye to the fascists: Perhaps Hitler and Mussolini were not so bad after all.

But in fact, World War II was already under way. As we shall shortly see, in Asia, Japan had already attacked China. In fascist Spain, General Francisco Franco, with the help of Hitler and Mussolini, was fighting the democratic government.

Americans, with great oceans protecting them from these events, were determined to stay out of foreign wars. Many were pacifists by belief; others were *isolationists,* convinced that the United States ought to mind its own business as much as possible. Still others felt that the United States had gone to war once to bail out the European democracies, all for naught, and ought not to do it again. True, some Americans felt that in time we would have to fight the fascists, among them President Franklin D. Roosevelt, who believed the nation would have to get involved sooner or later, as we shall see. But most were opposed to another fight with Germany.

Hitler, therefore quite shrewdly concluded that the democracies would not stop him. He continued to build up Germany's military forces, and declared that the nation needed more "living space" for its overcrowded people. He therefore instituted a policy of nibbling away at the lands around him. He first eyed Austria. There was considerable support for the Nazi movement in this German-speaking nation. Indeed, a lot of Austrians felt that they would be well advised to become part of Germany. In 1938 Hitler massed troops on the Austrian border and demanded that an Austrian Nazi be put in charge of the Austrian government. He was; the German army moved in, and Austria came under Hitler's control.

Hitler had already begun his attacks on Jews in Germany. They were fired from government jobs, often had their businesses taken from them, were beaten by Nazi thugs, sometimes arrested. Many of them fled to other nations; but many others stayed. Now it was the turn of the Austrian Jews to suffer; many of them also fled, but others, unfortunately for them, stayed.

Next, Hitler turned toward Czechoslovakia (in 1993 divided into the Czech Republic and Slovakia). The western end of this nation, the Sudetenland, contained a great many people of German descent. Hitler demanded the right to annex (take over) the Sudetenland. The French and English announced that they would support Czechoslovakia. Armies mobilized. In the end, however, the prime minister of England, Neville Chamberlain, made a deal with Hitler: If the Germans would promise to

make no more territorial demands, Hitler could have the Sudetenland. The French went along. Chamberlain announced to great acclaim that he had gained "peace in our time." This "appeasement" of Hitler was soon seen as a cowardly cave-in, but at the time the democracies were jubilant at having avoided war.

But they had not. In March 1939 Hitler marched his troops into Czechoslovakia and took over the whole nation. Too late, France and England began frantically building up their military forces.

In the United States public opinion was steadfastly antiwar. As an expression of the pacifist sentiments engendered by the failure of World War I to secure democracy in Europe, Congress passed a series of "neutrality acts" in the 1930s. These acts forbade Americans—including the government—from aiding any nation at war by selling them arms or lending them money to buy them. Many Americans believed that they had been dragged into World War I by munitions makers and bankers who had too much at stake in an Allied victory. They did not want this to happen again.

These neutrality acts prevented the United States from helping the democratic government during the Spanish Civil War or the Ethiopian spearmen against whom Mussolini had sent tanks and airplanes in an effort to build an Italian empire in 1935.

In 1937 Roosevelt had suggested that these fascist dictators should be isolated and denied essential trade. The public outcry against this hint of involvement in European affairs had been so great that he did not press his belief that the United States should be preparing for war. But publicly, President Roosevelt supported noninvolvement, all the time knowing that sooner or later the United States would have to get into the coming war to stop Hitler. By 1939 a growing number of Americans was coming to the same conclusion; but the majority wanted to stay out.

Hitler was now convinced that the democracies would never fight to stop him, and he set his sights on Poland. This unhappy nation, in medieval times a power in Central Europe, had been pulled apart again and again by Russia, Germany, and Hungary. Hitler knew that Russia

The Germans began their attack on Poland with waves of these Stuka dive-bombers, which proved very effective against ground troops. They were also used, however, against civilian refugees fleeing the war along country roads.

Left: A Polish citizen being searched by German soldiers. Civilians were not supposed to carry arms, and might be shot for doing so.

Below: Jews were rounded up by Hitler's elite forces at Warsaw and elsewhere. Some were confined to ghettos, some sent off to labor or death camps. In the end, few of Poland's Jews survived.

would not stand idly by while he swallowed Poland. In 1939 he made a secret pact with the Russian dictator, Joseph Stalin, not to fight each other, but to divide up Poland when the time came.

When this deal came out the world was stunned. After all, Hitler was an avowed anti-communist. Nonetheless, it was clear that Hitler aimed to take over Poland. This time the British and French knew they would have to fight, and they declared that they would. Hitler didn't believe them. The armies began to mobilize, and on September 1, the Germans marched into Poland. Two days later, France and England declared war against Germany. World War II was truly begun.

CHAPTER II

The World Goes to War

The German army swept through unhappy Poland in a month, despite valorous fighting by the Poles. The Russians came in from the east, and very soon Poland was divided.

Meanwhile, the British and French delayed an aggressive counterattack. It is true that both nations had hoped desperately that war could be avoided, and were not as well prepared for it as they should have been. Nonetheless, it is now clear to historians that, with the bulk of the German army hundreds of miles away fighting in Poland, the French alone could have easily swept into Germany from the west, and stopped World War II before it started. The British, too, although weak in some respects, had a strong force of bombers that could have flown over Germany unmolested while the German air force was operating in Poland. True, Hitler's propaganda had convinced the world that its forces were far stronger than they actually were. Democratic governments have to listen to public opinion and in France and England public opinion was still strongly against war; the democratic allies held back.

For the moment things in Europe were quiet. After their quick victory in Poland the Germans began to prepare for the next phase in the war, without restraint by the British or French. Then, in April 1940, the Germans suddenly struck into Norway and Denmark. Both countries had hoped to stay out of the war; neither had much of an army, and both were quickly taken. The Germans never attacked Sweden, allowing it to remain "neutral," but controlled it anyway.

By this time Winston Churchill had risen in the British government, and was rapidly growing in influence. Churchill had been head of the British navy during World War I, and had been one of the few influential Englishmen who had wanted to take a stronger stand against Hitler. For taking this position he had been kept out of power; but now that events were proving him right, people were increasingly listening to his

Before mounting their attack on France, the Germans swept into Denmark and Norway in order to prevent an attack from the north. Neither country had a large military force and both were quickly subdued. Here, Germans guard a port on Norway's long coast.

advice. With the fall of Norway, about which the British were able to do nothing, Neville Chamberlain was finally discredited. He resigned and Churchill became prime minister. It was a case of a man whose time had come. Winston Churchill would become one of the greatest war heroes in British history.

Almost immediately Churchill had a real war on his hands. In May 1940 the Germans attacked France in a campaign that an authoritative historian has called "one of the world's great military masterpieces." The French had expected the Germans to attack through Belgium, and in fact the Germans did drive a force into that hapless nation. But the main German thrust came farther south, through the thick Ardennes Forest, which the French had considered impassable. While French and British armies fought in Belgium, the Germans poured through the Ardennes,

A rare photo, taken by an official German army photographer, shows the German army on the attack. The Germans caught the French by surprise with their attack through the Ardennes Forest and swept into Paris.

Another official German photograph showing the German infantry moving forward.

aiming directly for Paris. They burst across the French line of defense at the Meuse River, and rolled into the heart of France. In truth, the Germans knew they were undermanned, and that their army was stretched thin to the breaking point. Had the French been able to gather their forces and make a concerted effort they might have halted the Germans then and there. But their leadership was confused and uncertain, paralyzed by the rapid German attack. The French government agreed to let Hitler take over the half of France occupied by German troops, while Frenchmen continued to govern the rest as a "puppet nation." Their new capital was the small city of Vichy; thus the unoccupied area was called Vichy France.

At this point the Italian dictator, Benito Mussolini, sensing a German victory, jumped into the fight on Hitler's side in order to share in the spoils. French morale collapsed, and within weeks France surrendered. The British were lucky to get the bulk of their troops back to England. This extraordinary withdrawal of about 250,000 soldiers from the

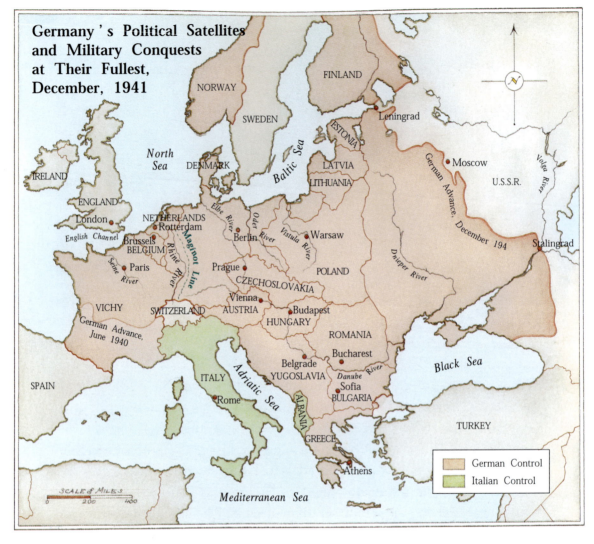

Germany's Political Satellites
and Military Conquests
at Their Fullest,
December, 1941

German Control
Italian Control

SCALE of MILES
0   200   400

beaches of Dunkirk across the English Channel was the one ray of sun-
shine in the darkness for the Allies.

Then, in June 1941, despite his peace agreement with Russia, Hitler
attacked that huge nation. The attack on Russia, when the Germans had
not yet defeated England, today seems foolhardy, and in the end would
prove disastrous for Germany. But victory after victory had convinced
Hitler that he was invincible and at first, as the German army raced into
the Russian heartland, it seemed that he was right.

Back in the United States, Americans were viewing these events with alarm. President Roosevelt had been convinced for two or three years that the United States would have to come into the war in Europe sooner or later, but the majority of Americans were still determined to stay out of it. Roosevelt had another serious concern—the ambitions of the Japanese halfway around the world. Once again we must step back a little to understand events in Asia.

For hundreds of years European nations had been trading in the Far East for spices, silk, tea, and other things. In time, with their greater military power, the British, Dutch, and French in particular, were able to take over many Asian nations, such as Cambodia, Indonesia, Vietnam, and many more, running them as colonies. In the 1800s the Americans got in on the game, colonizing Hawaii, the Philippines, and some smaller islands. The point was to get raw materials like rubber, rice, timber, and much else from the colonies, and to use the colonies as markets for European manufactured goods, like cloth and machines. In addition, coal could be deposited at places like Hawaii to fuel the large steam-powered navies the great imperial powers needed to control their colonies.

However, the Chinese and Japanese resisted the European exploitation. The Chinese would allow Europeans to establish trading posts only at a few points along the coast; the Japanese would not let Europeans in at all. But by the mid-1800s, the more powerful Europeans and Americans were able to force China and Japan to open their lands to trade.

The Japanese now made a sharp about-face: they would keep their ancient culture, but they would copy the Western technological advances, like warships, modern rifles, cameras, chemicals, heavy machinery, and eventually planes and trucks. The problem with this scheme was that the Japanese had few of the raw materials, like iron ore, rubber, and oil, that were needed for a modern industrial system. Most of the sources of such raw materials in Asia were in the hands of Western colonists—oil in

Indonesia, rubber in British Malaya, rice in the American Philippines. The Japanese greedily eyed these colonies covetously.

There was psychology as well as practicality involved, too. The Japanese believed that they were an important people with an old culture, and were superior to the rough "barbarians" from the West. They had, as well, a militaristic culture that vastly admired the warrior hero and the willingness to die in battle for the nation. They resented Western military might, and wanted to play the larger role in the world they felt entitled to. They sided with England and France in World War I and took some Asian colonies from Germany. By the 1920s the Japanese were determined to make themselves the primary power in Asia, taking what they needed from the lands around them by assumed right.

The situation in China was different. That nation, too, had an ancient culture. It was, however, a very large nation, difficult to govern effectively, and had, over the centuries, seen many changes of government. During the nineteenth century, China had begun to Westernize itself to an extent. It had developed particularly strong trading relationships with the United States. Still, its government was ineffective; and by the early 1930s a Communist faction, led by Mao Zedong, was battling a nationalist faction friendly to the West led by Jiang Jieshi (formerly spelled Chiang Kei-shek), with each side controlling portions of the vast nation.

In September 1931 the Japanese took over the section of China called Manchuria, and installed its own "puppet" government there. The United States protested; so did the League of Nations and other democracies. But in 1931 the United States was not about to get itself into a war in this strange, faraway place. In 1933 Japan withdrew from the League of Nations, a signal that it was on an aggressive path, and in 1937 invaded China. The major port city of Shanghai soon fell to the Japanese and a little later so did Nanking, then China's capital.

There is no getting around the fact that the Japanese behaved with terrible viciousness in the war with China. In Nanking, Japanese troops raped 80,000 women and slaughtered over a quarter of a million civilians. They also subjected Shanghai to massive bombing. Later on, massive bombing of cities full of women and children would be practiced by all of the combatants in World War II, but at the time the Japanese bombing of Shanghai and other places horrified Americans. Americans tended to be sympathetic to the Chinese due to old trading ties, and increasingly Americans came to see the Japanese as a potential enemy. Still, nobody was ready to fight: The isolationists warned against trying "to police a world that chooses to follow insane leaders."

By 1938 Japan controlled most of China's ports. Americans were alarmed, and Roosevelt sent what aid he could to China, pushed for a

This famous picture shows a crying Chinese baby in the ruins of Shanghai after a Japanese bombing raid. The bombing of Shanghai was one of the first mass attacks on civilians, and horrified many people. Far worse was to come.

buildup of the American navy, and began to curtail sales of raw materials, machinery, and other essential items to Japan, which was buying much of what it needed from the United States.

But the Japanese were determined to become the dominant power in Asia, and they pressed ahead. By 1940, with the German army victorious in Europe, Japan realized that the Dutch, French, and Belgians could not defend their Asian colonies. The Japanese government demanded concessions from the Europeans. In September 1940 they signed the so-called Tripartite Pact, joining Germany and Italy to make three "Axis Powers." Changes in the Japanese government brought in even more aggressive leaders, especially war minister Hideki Tojo.

Roosevelt continued to press America to prepare for the war he was sure was coming. He got Congress to authorize the expenditure of what was at the time a huge sum of money to more than double the size of the navy. And in September 1940, he persuaded Congress to pass the Selective Training and Service bill, under which men would be drafted into the United States military—the first peacetime draft in American history. Over the next year hundreds of thousands of young men found themselves in uniform, learning how to service fighter planes, scrub decks, kill with bayonets. The same month Roosevelt also made a deal to lend Britain fifty retired destroyers in exchange for a lease on nearby British naval bases in the Caribbean Sea—the famous Lend-Lease deal. The United States was clearly no longer neutral; it would do what it could to help the Allies, short of fighting.

Roosevelt believed that the rampaging Germans represented a greater danger to the world than the Japanese, but the Japanese threat was very real. The Americans had cracked Japan's secret code, and by the middle of 1941 American officials knew that the Japanese were planning to strike somewhere in the Pacific after mid-November. Where, they did not know.

Roosevelt now decided to cut off American oil from the Japanese. The Japanese could not continue the war in China, much less fight any-

An official army painting, drawn from life, shows young American men arriving at an army camp after they had been drafted.

where else, without oil. They began trying to negotiate with the Americans; but they were also getting ready to fight. The Americans guessed that they would hit at some place in Southeast Asia, like the Dutch colony of Indonesia, with its rich oil fields, or perhaps the Philippine Islands. Nonetheless, the Navy Department in Washington was deeply worried about Pearl Harbor, the great American naval port at Honolulu in Hawaii, where much of the American Pacific fleet was based. It warned the commanders of a possible Japanese strike there.

At seven o'clock on the morning of Sunday, December 7, 1941, two army privates, Joe Lockhard and George Elliot, were manning a radar unit on the north end of Hawaii's main island. They saw suddenly appear on the screen a huge blip, larger than anything they had ever seen before. Astonished, Lockhard checked the equipment to see if everything was working correctly. It was. He called his headquarters and reported that a large number of planes was coming in from the north. Nobody took him seriously; it must be a mistake. But at 7:55 a mass of Japanese planes, launched from aircraft carriers out at sea, roared over the totally unprepared Americans, bombing and strafing at will. Japanese submarines slipped into Pearl Harbor and unleashed their torpedoes. For two hours the planes shot up ships, airports, supply depots. When they were finished, eight battleships had been sunk or badly damaged, 2,403 Americans were dead, hundreds of planes were destroyed. For the Americans, the only bright side to Pearl Harbor was

Yet another famous picture shows an American navy ship burning after the attack on Pearl Harbor by the Japanese on December 7, 1941.

that no American aircraft carriers happened to be in Pearl Harbor that morning. That lucky break would make a difference very soon.

Ever since that fateful day, people have wondered how the United States could have been so taken by surprise. Why were all those ships so neatly lined up in Pearl Harbor, like ducks in a shooting gallery, instead of dispersed at sea? Why didn't anyone believe Joe Lockhard's radar report and send American planes up to meet the Japanese? Some people have even suggested that Roosevelt knew the attack on Pearl Harbor was coming, and deliberately withheld the information, so as to draw the United States into the war against Germany, although few historians accept this idea.

In part the problem was an old one—the wish people have to look on the bright side. Of course, many Americans still viewed World War I as one in which the United States had been duped into bailing out the corrupt old European imperialist nations. Public opinion did not permit the government to gear up for war nor were Depression-poor taxpayers willing to pay for it. Military posts were not generally on a standby status. But still, part of the problem at Pearl Harbor was sheer human error: In the days leading up to Pearl Harbor a lot of people made mistakes. Finally, some credit must be given to the Japanese: They had come up with a sound plan and had executed it brilliantly. Whatever the case, on that December morning the world changed forever. Roosevelt, calling it a "date which will live in infamy," asked Congress for a declaration of war, not just against the Japanese, but against the other Axis powers as well. It was now indeed a world war.

The failure of the public and their representatives in Congress to wake up to the Japanese threat and the resulting lack of military preparedness taught Americans a lesson they would apply after World War II was over. Keeping the United States' defenses strong, and paying the price in tax dollars, became a dominating political concern throughout the second half of the twentieth century.

CHAPTER III

Americans Begin to Fight

World War II lasted, if we count the Japanese invasion of China as the start, for eight years, and was fought all over the globe. It is a huge story, and we can only touch on the highlights of it in a book of this size.

We will concentrate on the role of the United States. We need to remember, however, that the Russians were fighting a bloody war against the Germans; that the British, Canadians, Australians, and New Zealanders had been in the war for two years before the Americans came in; and that exiled soldiers from Germany's victims, like the French, Dutch, and Belgians, also fought and died alongside the Allies.

In fact, America's work of supplying its allies with the tools of war may have been as important to ultimate victory as the actual fighting done by American soldiers and sailors. Without American oil, planes, food, and much else, England and Russia could not have held out against the Germans.

The Germans, of course, knew this, but before Pearl Harbor they had been careful about attacking American shipping, fearful of drawing the United States into the war as they had in World War I. Now that the

United States was in, German submarines were free to attack American ships. The nation was ill-equipped to fend off submarine attacks. The German subs began to range within eyesight of the American coast. One submarine, patrolling off New York Harbor in 1942, sank eight American ships in twelve hours. Another one surfaced in sight of Jacksonville Beach, Florida, and sank an American tanker with its deck gun. The sub was so close to shore that through his binoculars the captain could see tourists on the beach watching the flaming tanker go down. By June 1942, 4.7 million tons of shipping had been sunk by the Germans, costing the Allies not only the ships, but the supplies they were carrying and the lives of many merchant seamen. The United States was losing more ships than it could build, and its allies were desperate for supplies.

America's first problem at the beginning of the war was to combat the German submarines lurking off the coast, where they were sinking a huge number of American transport ships. In this picture, depth charges, which could destroy a submarine if they exploded nearby, are being launched from the deck of a ship. This painting, like others in this book, was made by an official military painter who had observed the action firsthand.

The Germans also had their military artists. This painting was captioned by the Germans, "Surprising fire from Allies on German tanks." It shows the war in the North African desert.

The United States began building small ships and fast airplanes designed specifically to attack subs. It also developed the system of sending goods to England and Russia in huge convoys of scores of ships, defended by escorts of destroyers. With sub losses mounting, the Germans pulled back to the mid-Atlantic, and while German subs continued to sink Allied ships until the end of the war, most of the supplies now got through.

At the outset, President Roosevelt had agreed with the leaders of his primary allies, Winston Churchill of England and Joseph Stalin of Russia, that the fight against Germany would get priority over the war against Japan. Even the Japanese understood that they could not successfully attack the United States itself: Their intention was simply to control the lands of the Far East. However, should Hitler defeat either England or Russia, he could soon defeat the other one. Thereafter it would be impossible to dislodge him from Europe, and he could turn his attention elsewhere. The Allies had to be kept in the fight; Japan could be dealt with later. (In fact, as we shall shortly see, the United States began pressing the war against Japan surprisingly quickly.)

Stalin was particularly desperate for the English and Americans to launch a "second front" against Germany in the west, to reduce the pressure on Russia. Roosevelt and the American generals agreed: They wanted to make a direct attack in France as soon as possible. Winston Churchill, remembering the trench fighting that had wiped out a whole generation of young men, persuaded Roosevelt that the Allies were not yet strong enough. However, something had to be done, not just to ease the pressure on Russia, but to give the people in the Allied nations the sense that they were going on the attack.

The British were already fighting the Germans in the deserts of North Africa, both to keep control of the Suez Canal, a crucial shipping route, and to hold the Germans out of the rich oil fields of the Mideast. The fighting had seesawed back and forth along the North African coast; it was now agreed by the top civil and military leaders that an invasion of the area might secure it for the Allies, and capture tens of thousands of German troops as well. An American general, Dwight D. Eisenhower, was picked to command the operation.

Two of the main leaders of the Allied war effort, British prime minister Winston Churchill and American general Dwight Eisenhower, who led the Allied forces in North Africa and then in Europe.

"Ike" Eisenhower would become the biggest American "star" of the war—so big, that on the strength of his victories he was eventually elected president. Born in Texas, the son of a railroad worker, he grew up in Abilene, Kansas, in modest circumstances. Although his mother was a pacifist, he entered the U.S. Military Academy at West Point and rose rapidly through the ranks during World War I, although he never saw combat. However, he eventually caught the eye of a general who thought he saw something in Eisenhower. Ike was sent off to a special school for higher officers, where he was first in his class, then became an assistant to the already famous General Douglas MacArthur in the Philippines.

When the war in Europe broke out, Eisenhower was brought to Washington for important jobs, impressing Chief of Staff General George C. Marshall. In 1942 he was given command of the growing American forces in England. Eisenhower, however, was something of a rarity in the army, a man who had risen to high place despite the fact that he had never been in combat, had never commanded even a small unit in battle. Yet his superiors were almost always struck by his intelligence, poise, and modesty. Although later other generals he worked with questioned his decisions on some matters, military historians have usually given him high marks for his generalship in World War II.

The invasion of North Africa was to be a two-pronged attack, hitting at Morocco at the center of the Atlantic coast and Algiers to the east. Initially the invasion was a breathtaking success: British and American troops very quickly took the areas assigned to them and linked up. However, the Germans still held Tunisia, only a short distance from the Italian island of Sicily. German reinforcements poured in from Sicily, and in February 1943 the Germans attacked. American troops were inexperienced. The Germans struck at these green troops at a place in Tunisia called Kasserine Pass. The Germans roared at them in force. One regiment of Americans was wiped out; so was the armored regiment that counterattacked. (An infantry regiment consists of about 3,000 men.)

Another rare German army photo. This one appeared in a German magazine during the war and was captioned, "An American Boston Bomber has crashed to the ground in flames." Actually, it was a P-38 fighter plane.

The Germans raced through the broken American forces, driving them back seventy miles. American tanks proved to be no match for the heavier German ones.

However, the German attack ran out of steam. The Americans pulled themselves together, and began to push the Germans back. The Battle of Kasserine Pass was a small one in the total picture, but it gave the Americans their first combat experience, curbed typical American optimism, and taught them that there would be hard fighting ahead.

Nonetheless, by April 1943, the Germans were being squeezed hard between the Americans and the British. Some managed to get across to Sicily, but a quarter of a million German and Italian troops were captured. At last the Allies had gained a substantial victory. The Germans, among other things, no longer commanded the Mediterranean Sea, a major transportation route for war materials.

As a look at a map will show, an attack on Sicily was the obvious next move. Taking Sicily would help clear the Mediterranean, and would also show the Russians that the Americans and British were on their way to opening a second front in Europe. Once again under Eisenhower's command, in July 1943 the Allies landed on Sicily. There was hard fighting, but in a little over a month they forced the defenders to escape into Italy.

Now what? The Americans still wanted an early direct attack on France, but Churchill argued for an invasion of Italy. Even if only the southern part of the Italian boot were captured, it would give the Allies a jumping-off point for their bombers and possible further invasions. The

The fighting was particularly bitter in Italy, where there was a long chain of mountains to be fought over. Here a soldier lies dead on Mount Altuzzo. We can see the rugged mountains behind, where much fighting was done.

The North African and Italian Campaigns

LANDINGS AT:
A Sicily --------------------------- July 1943
B Reggio and Salerno ----------- September 1943
C Anzio ----------------------- January 1944

Axes Surrender
May 1943

Americans gave in. As it happened, the Italians were thoroughly sick of what they saw as Hitler's war. They also were sick of Mussolini. Hitler realized this, and he began sending German troops into Italy to hold the Italians firm. Nonetheless, Italian leaders persuaded the king, who had at least official authority though no real power, to fire Mussolini which he did. Then, Mussolini was arrested, escaped with German help, but was caught again by underground Italian forces. Mussolini and his girlfriend were executed by machine gun, and their bodies hung upside down from a lamppost, a scene that all the world would see in a photograph that was reproduced everywhere.

The Italians were now out of the war, and the Allies, as they advanced, found themselves fighting the much tougher Germans. Part of the problem was that, increasingly, American resources were going to the war in the Pacific, about which we shall hear more shortly. Other men and matériel were going to England for the upcoming invasion of France.

Another problem was the terrain: Rugged, twisting mountains ran up the center of much of the Italian peninsula, making formidable defensive positions.

Nonetheless, the initial landings were successful, and the Americans pushed forward. Then they slowed. The Germans dug in behind the many rivers that ran across Italy to the sea; the Allies would drive them out after much hard, deadly fighting, only to find them dug in again behind another river. But slowly, the Allies pushed forward.

A key point on the road north to Rome was the town of Cassino. Above the town on top of a mountain was a famous ancient monastery. Try as they might, the Americans could not batter their way past Cassino. It was decided, then, to land troops on the coast farther north at a place called Anzio. The idea was to push rapidly across the Italian boot, cutting off the German troops from behind, and perhaps forcing a large-scale surrender. The landing caught the Germans by surprise, but they quickly rallied and contained the threat. For weeks the Allied troops sat in their little beachhead, pounded by German fire, unable to move forward.

Finally, the high command realized that more resources had to be sent to Italy. A large-scale campaign was mounted, and Allied troops broke out at Anzio and Cassino, took Rome, and began to push north. But now the invasion of France was looming ahead. Allied troops were called back to Britain, and not until the war was over was Italy finally conquered.

When we talk about war in a book like this one we must view it at large, as if it were a chess game. But we must not forget that war is fought by human beings, usually in the most unpleasant circumstances. The ordinary combat soldier, besides facing death without relief for days, or even weeks, at a stretch, was never sure of a good night's sleep, was often exhausted, wet through to the skin, freezing in the mountains of Italy or sweating in the baking, mosquito-infested heat of a Pacific island. The United States army was famous for seeing that its troops were well supplied, but even so, a man in the midst of combat was often hungry,

The war was finally brought home to Germany with bombing raids on German cities. This painting, made by a German artist on the spot, shows Berlin after an air raid. Civilians, bombed out of their homes, seek shelter.

thirsty, and almost always tired. Then, as he came out of a dreadful day's fighting, he had to deal with the fact that some of his friends lay dead in the snow or the mud, their brains blown out, their intestines spread in the dirt. Airmen and sailors had it better in some ways, for most of the time they were able to sleep in warm, dry quarters, however cramped, and eat reasonable meals. But then they, too, would face the desperate moments when the world around them was on fire, explosive shells tearing at them.

Yet despite the terror most men felt in combat, there were thousands of cases of heroism. During the Italian campaign an African-American, Lieutenant Vernon Baker, took his platoon on an attack of a German mountain strong point. He crawled into a bunker and killed its two defenders, killed two more in a machine-gun nest, blew open another bunker and machine-gunned the occupants. Baker won a Distinguished

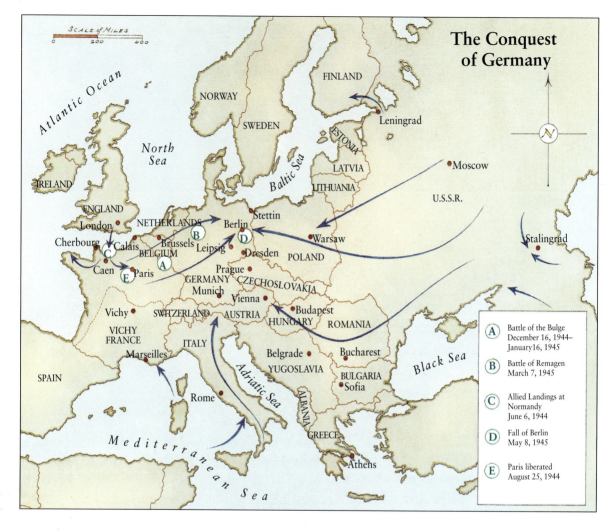

The Conquest
of Germany

SCALE OF MILES
0   200   400

Atlantic Ocean

North
Sea

Baltic Sea

Mediterranean Sea

Adriatic Sea

Black Sea

IRELAND
ENGLAND
London
Cherbourg
Calais
Caen
Paris
Brussels
NETHERLANDS
BELGIUM
Leipsig
Berlin
Stettin
Dresden
Prague
GERMANY
Munich
Vienna
Budapest
AUSTRIA
HUNGARY
ROMANIA
SWITZERLAND
Vichy
VICHY
FRANCE
ITALY
Marseilles
SPAIN
Rome
Belgrade
YUGOSLAVIA
BULGARIA
Sofia
ALBANIA
GREECE
Athens
Bucharest
POLAND
Warsaw
CZECHOSLOVAKIA
LITHUANIA
LATVIA
ESTONIA
FINLAND
NORWAY
SWEDEN
Leningrad
Moscow
U.S.S.R.
Stalingrad

N

A Battle of the Bulge
December 16, 1944–
January 16, 1945

B Battle of Remagen
March 7, 1945

C Allied Landings at
Normandy
June 6, 1944

D Fall of Berlin
May 8, 1945

E Paris liberated
August 25, 1944

Service Medal for this action, which was later upgraded to a Congressional Medal of Honor.

The landing of Allied troops on the beaches of Normandy, France, in June 1944, is one of the greatest stories in all military history. It has been told countless times in books, movies, plays, magazines. It was, indeed, a dramatic event, and tragic for the thousands of men who died in it.

The first question was where to attack. The English Channel, which divides the British Isles from France, can be very rough in bad weather, and it was first thought to make for the shortest crossing, landing at

Soldiers on the Normandy beaches on D-Day, June 6, 1944. Once again, this painting was made by an official military artist who observed the action.

Calais. However, vast quantities of men and matériel would have to be landed, so it was decided to invade near a good-sized port. The port city of Cherbourg, on a point of land jutting out into the English Channel, farther down the French coast in the province of Normandy, was chosen.

The critical moment in an invasion from the sea is the time when the invaders come in unprotected in small boats, and then must cross exposed beaches. Making matters worse, at many points along the coast near Cherbourg steep cliffs rose up from the sea, which the invaders would have to climb. It was decided to risk it.

After his successes in North Africa and Sicily, Dwight Eisenhower was the logical choice for commander. Under "Ike," a plan was developed that called for parachute and glider troops to land before the sea landings to disrupt German transportation and communications behind the lines. The Germans were well aware that the invasion was coming, but Hitler was convinced that the Allies would land in the Calais area. It was a costly mistake. Early in the morning of June 6, 1944,—D-Day—the parachutists plunged into Normandy, and began driving the Germans from small villages and towns there, taking control of roads where they could. At daybreak the small landing vessels began to run troops ashore. Some of them had relatively easy going; but at the code-named Omaha Beach, the Americans had a fight on their hands. Here a steep bluff rose up from the sands, and on the bluff was a tough, experienced German force. Many Americans died in the landing boats coming in, others on the beaches. Demoralized and scattered, for a time it was touch-and-go. But gradually the soldiers went forward, dashing across the sand to the base of the bluff in small groups, sometimes alone. Slowly they clambered up the cliff, taking fearful losses, but by nightfall they were at the top and driving the Germans back.

The invaders were aided by two conditions. For one, after years of heavy fighting the German air force was almost finished; the invaders had clear skies above them. For another, during the first crucial hours Hitler continued to believe that the attack was a feint, and that the real invasion would still come at Calais. He held the reserves back until the Allies had gotten their foothold.

The Normandy invasion produced many heroes. One was Harrison Summers, a paratroop sergeant from West Virginia, who dropped into Normandy. On landing, he was given fifteen men he'd never seen before, and told to take out about a hundred German artillery men stationed in stone farm buildings along a road in back of the beach. Shouting for the men to follow him, he charged the first of the farm buildings. When he got to the door he discovered he was alone: His men were hidden down in a ditch. Summers kicked open the door and machine-gunned the four Germans there. Now one of his squad began to support him with rifle fire. Summers ran on to the next farmhouse and once again machine-gunned the Germans, killing six of them. At the third farmhouse the Germans quickly surrendered. Two of the squad joined Summers. They raced from one farmhouse to the next, in the process killing thirty more Germans. In all, Summers and his two men killed fifty-one Germans and captured thirty-one. Afterwards Summers was asked how he felt. "Not very good," he said. "It was kind of crazy." That was often the case in heroic actions like these: The men were unable to explain the emotions that moved them. Summers was awarded the Distinguished Service Cross for his action.

But the Germans were far from through. The Allies had expected to take the key city of Caen the first day of the invasion and in two weeks or so to have fought their way into Cherbourg, the port they needed. Only bit by bit did the Allies gain ground. Among other things, the hedgerows that crisscrossed the countryside were not simple hedges, but thickly matted, tall walls of saplings set in dirt parapets (low walls), which made formidable defensive lines. The Allied troops had to fight across this land foot by foot. But by late June they had thirty-four divisions ashore—about a half million men—along with massive amounts of equipment. The Germans continued to fight hard, but by late July they were outnumbered and outgunned. The Allies made a desperate push, and suddenly they broke through.

Now began one of the great stories of the war. Among the American forces was the 3rd U.S. Army (an army is made up of several divisions of 10,000 to 15,000 men), commanded by the swaggering General George Patton. At the beginning of August, Patton started racing his tanks and armored trucks southwest. In the first three days of August they gained seventy-five miles, an extraordinary distance in a war. This daring drive confused the Germans, and they began to fall back in disorder. The Allies now pressed forward all along the front, rapidly gaining ground. A group under the British Field Marshall Bernard Montgomery drove through Belgium and into Holland, taking the important port of Antwerp before the Germans could demolish it. By the fall of 1944, Paris had been taken, and much of the Low Countries and France were in Allied hands. The Germans had lost hundreds of thousands of men and huge amounts of supplies. Allied bombers were blasting German cities and their factories. To the east, the Russians were driving toward the German borders. The Allies were now poised to push into Germany itself. But for the moment they were forced to slow down, in order to rest the exhausted troops and build up their supplies.

For the Germans the war was clearly lost and, in July 1944, some German officers attempted to kill Hitler. The plot failed, and Hitler replaced many officers with those he knew would be loyal to him. He was determined to fight on. For one thing, the Germans were now producing the first-ever jet fighters: All planes used in the war until this point had been driven by propellers. For another, the Germans also had a new device, the jet-propelled rocket bombs, the first real missiles, with which they were hitting London. Perhaps the Allies could yet be halted.

But despite the might of the Allied armies, there was a weak point in the area of the Ardennes Forest—the same place where the Germans had thrust into France five years earlier. Here the Allied line was stretched thin, and many of the troops were green and inexperienced. Suddenly, on the morning of December 16, 1944, the Germans struck with a large force into the Ardennes. The green American troops reeled backwards, with small units of men wandering the snow-covered forests trying to find their commands. The Germans then headed for a road junction at a little town called Bastogne. They had now driven a wedge sixty miles into the Allied lines. The Americans rushed the 101st Airborne Division into Bastogne. They were told to hold it at all costs. The Germans surrounded the 101st at Bastogne and demanded a surrender. The American General Anthony MacAuliffe responded simply, "Nuts."

Unfortunately for the Americans, heavy clouds prevented their planes from helping at Bastogne. Still, the Germans could not push through. The day after Christmas, the clouds blew away. American planes attacked the Germans on the ground, Allied reinforcements came up, and slowly the Germans were driven back. Six weeks after this famous Battle of the Bulge began, the Germans were back where they had started, but with

The Germans made a last desperate thrust into Allied lines in December 1944, but a determined American force held them up at the little town of Bastogne. Soon the Germans were pushed back, and the famous Battle of the Bulge was over.

200,000 fewer troops and most of what had remained of their air force wrecked.

One of the most famous American heroes of World War II came out of the Battle of the Bulge. Lieutenant Audie Murphy, the twenty-one-year-old son of a poor sharecropper from Texas, was told to hold a certain position with a very small force. He and his eighteen men and two tank destroyers were attacked by two hundred Germans with six heavy tanks. One of Murphy's tank destroyers got stuck in a ditch, the other was hit by German fire. Murphy pulled his men back into a patch of woods and held off the Germans until ammunition ran out. He then ran forward to his crippled tank and raked the advancing Germans with its machine gun. Next he called down artillery fire on his own position to stop oncoming German tanks, and raced away. The German attack was stopped. Murphy engaged in other acts of great bravery and became the most decorated American soldier of the war.

On the Eastern Front the Russians were now driving into Germany itself, drawing off German troops from the Western Front. By March, the Allies had reached the Rhine River, where they intended to pause to plan the crossing. The Germans blew up the Rhine bridges, confident that they could make the Allies pay a heavy price for the crossing.

Then, on the morning of March 7, 1945, two American privates, Charlie Penrod and Ralph Munch, were scouting along a road through a wooded area, looking cautiously for signs of the enemy. As they moved up the road, the Rhine suddenly came into view. To their vast astonishment, a short way up the river they saw an intact bridge across the Rhine at the little town of Remagen. They raced back to their commander, Second Lieutenant Karl Timmermann, to report the news. Timmermann knew that as soon as the Germans sighted Americans they'd blow up the bridge. He was ordered to take his company into Remagen. Quickly, Timmermann secured the town. By this time higher officers were aware that the Remagen Bridge was still intact. Timmermann's men began moving toward it. Suddenly there was a roar. The Germans had blown the bridge after all. Or so they thought, for when the roar died down, the bridge was still standing.

On the opposite end, in Germany, men with machine guns in twin towers protected the bridge. Orders came down to Timmermann: Take the bridge. Timmermann's men were aghast—charge across the bridge in the face of machine-gun fire from the towers at the other end? But those were the orders. Timmermann moved out onto the bridge, waving for his men to follow. A tank came up and blew out one of the towers. Huddling low, Timmermann's men moved cautiously forward.

The famous Remagen Bridge, looking east toward the German side. German machine gunners were in these towers when Lieutenant Timmermann and his men charged along the bridge and drove them out. Remagen was a railroad bridge: The tracks lead through a tunnel in the hill in the distance.

"Git goin', git goin'," Timmermann shouted. Bobbing and weaving, the men raced along the bridge into the machine-gun fire. Sergeant Joe Delisio reached the tower first. He kicked open the door at the base of the tower, raced up the stairs, captured the Germans there, and flung their machine gun out the window. By nightfall American troops were pouring across the Remagen Bridge into Germany. The Rhine had been crossed. Why had the Remagen Bridge not been blown apart? Nobody is sure, but it seemed likely that gunfire had by chance clipped the wires leading to some of the charges, so they never blew. Timmermann, too, was decorated for his extraordinary leadership and bravery.

There was still some heavy fighting to do, but with the Allies pressing them from the west and the Russians from the east, the Germans had little chance. Through April they fought a desperate, last-ditch battle, with old men and boys conscripted into the army. On May 1, Hitler, trapped

By 1945 the Germans were finished. Here the celebrated 82nd Airborne Division fights through the rubble of a German town.

in Berlin, committed suicide, and on May 8—called V-E Day for Victory in Europe—Germany surrendered. The war in Europe was over.

Only as the fighting ended did the world learn of the true evil of the Nazis. As Allied troops fought through Poland into Germany, they discovered terrible concentration camps, like the ones at Auschwitz and Buchenwald, where millions of people had been systematically murdered in batches. The victims included Catholics, homosexuals, Slavs, the retarded, political dissidents, gypsies, and others, but most of them were Jews, whom Hitler wished to totally eliminate from Europe. Now the victorious Allies found bodies stacked up like cordwood, piles of teeth broken from corpses for their gold fillings, death chambers where men, women, and children were gassed.

This slaughter of the Jews and others, generally called the Holocaust, has created much argument. What did the Allies know about it earlier, and could they have done anything to stop it? Was it mainly the work of the Nazis, or did ordinary Germans support it? We cannot, in a short space, discuss these questions in detail: Students interested in the Holocaust will find plenty of material to look into. But there is no question that the Holocaust did happen, that millions of people, mostly Jews, were rounded up by the Germans, and in some cases, by the French, Poles, and others who were cooperating with their German conquerors. Not all of those sent to the death camps died there, but in the end six million Jews were killed in these camps, and other millions were slaughtered elsewhere. In Poland alone, the Jewish population was reduced from four million to a few thousand.

This painting by a military artist shows the bodies stacked up at the Buchenwald death camp, where many Jews, along with others, were slaughtered by the Germans. American troops were stunned when they came across the camps.

CHAPTER IV

The Home Front

Worked War II has sometimes been called a "total" war, because it involved not just soldiers, but many, if not most, of the civilians in the nations at war. People a thousand miles from the battlefields could die in bombing raids. Others saw their lives overturned as the enemy swept into their cities and towns, burnt their farmhouses, blew up the factories where they worked, and reduced them to poverty.

Of all the major combatants, only the Americans, protected by two oceans, escaped total war. The United States was never seriously threatened by the enemy, nor were American cities bombed the way London, Berlin, and Stalingrad were. A little over 10 percent of Americans actually served in the military, a little over one percent saw combat, about a third of one percent died in the war.

Nonetheless, although Americans escaped much of the horror of World War II, the war had a profound effect on American life, some of it even good. Perhaps most important, when the war began the United States was struggling against the Great Depression, then ten years old, which at times had seen 25 percent of Americans out of work, and most of the rest on low wages. Many children were going without shoes, proper food, and

56

clothes. (For the story of the Great Depression, see the volume in this series called *Progressivism, the Depression, and the New Deal*.)

As America began to supply the English, Russians, and Chinese with food and arms in 1940, the American industrial machine began to speed up. Once the United States entered the war, factories began working full blast, turning out ships, combat boots, rifles, airplanes. At the same time millions of men and some women were siphoned off by the military; now there were more jobs than there were people to fill them. Wages rose. People who for ten years had struggled to find even low-paying jobs, had worn patched clothes and eaten thin soup day after day, found them-

The war turned the United States into a huge "arsenal for democracy," as the term was. There were jobs for everybody. Here men are working on M-4 tanks in a Ford automobile factory that a year earlier was turning out cars.

selves with money in their pockets, new dresses, meat on the table, the electric refrigerators and toasters that previously only the well-to-do had owned. This sudden prosperity was, for most Americans, possibly the single most significant effect of World War II.

Unfortunately, as ever, the money was not always fairly distributed. Farmers, who had not seen good times for decades, were much better off, and so were laborers working overtime in war plants. Inevitably, the government turned to giant corporations like General Motors and U.S. Steel to produce the incredible flood of war supplies, along with ordinary civilian goods, that were needed. To encourage businesses to change from making cars to planes, suits to army uniforms, the government allowed most businesses to make large profits on war goods. As a result, many businessmen came out of the war rich. Congress tried to limit such profits by levying taxes as high as 91 percent on the very highest incomes, but even so, a lot of large corporation executives and owners of large factories who had struggled during the Great Depression became rich during the war.

The demand for labor affected all groups. Before the war, it was customary for wives, especially those with children, to stay at home. Though about half of all single women worked, mainly as household servants, nurses, teachers, secretaries, most quit their jobs when they married. Now the government began encouraging women to go into the war plants. The famous symbol of "Rosie the Riveter," still remembered today, was on posters everywhere. Actually, few women became riveters; most who went into factories worked at unskilled jobs. Eventually two million women, many of them married, did war work.

The military, too, began recruiting women into special branches of the services. Women were not sent into combat, but served as drivers, radio operators, nurses, doctors, and clerks, thus releasing men for combat duties. Eventually 300,000 women joined the military service.

African-Americans, too, benefited from the war. At the war's out-

Millions of women found jobs in factories doing work that had once only been done by men. Here a woman uses a torch to cut through steel.

break, most white Americans were, to one degree or another, prejudiced against African-Americans, or Negroes, as they were then called. Even those who thought that African-Americans ought to be treated better often did not want to associate with them. It is difficult for us today, used to seeing blacks earning big salaries in sports and entertainment, and holding important offices in government, to realize that in 1940 even famous African-American entertainers could not get rooms in good hotels or tables at good restaurants, and were required by law to sit in the back of buses and go to segregated schools in the southern states.

The prejudice against African-Americans held for the military, too: African-Americans in the navy could generally work only as cooks and waiters for officers; in the army, blacks were mostly assigned to labor battalions loading ships, trains, and the like.

Negro organizations fought against this color bar, demanding that African-Americans be fully integrated into the military to fight side by side with whites. The military resisted: Some officers felt that blacks lacked the discipline, indeed the courage, to make good soldiers. Others felt that white soldiers would resent having blacks living with them. This was undoubtedly true: Not all white Americans were prejudiced against blacks, but many were, especially whites from the South where African-Americans were segregated by law. Only very slowly were African-Americans included in the fighting, and usually they went into combat in their own units, often with white officers. The situation was not one the nation could be proud of; yet despite everything, the war did help lower the bars between the races. And after the war, the military step-by-step became racially integrated.

African-Americans also benefited from the great demand for labor. They had always been "last hired, first fired" by industry, and mainly worked at the most menial, poorest-paying jobs. But now industry began hiring African-Americans to work on the factory floor, and many found themselves with comfortable incomes for the first time in their lives.

With everybody included, and businessmen pushing hard because of the profits to be made, during the war the American industrial machine accomplished a miracle. Already the largest in the world, producing twice as much coal as Germany, ten times as many cars, it began to run at an astonishing rate. The first so-called Liberty Ship, built to transport supplies around the world, took 355 days to build in 1940; by 1943 ship-yards were turning them out in forty-one days. In all, 2,700 were made. By 1944 Ford's Willow Run plant was producing a huge B-24 bomber every sixty-three minutes. By the war's end the nation had built 299,293 planes, 634,569 jeeps, forty *billion* bullets. And yet at the same time, the production of civilian goods increased by 12 percent. The importance of this miracle of production must not be underestimated. Without it, the Allies simply could not have won the war.

There were, nonetheless, shortages on the home front. Virtually all of the raw material for rubber came from Asia, which the Japanese soon controlled. America quickly expanded synthetic rubber production, but this was needed for the military, so tires were rationed. Gasoline, too, was rationed; so were butter, meat, sugar, bicycles, and many other items. Ration boards, made up of local citizens, handed out books of ration stamps to families according to the number of family members. Housewives shopping in butcher shops and grocery stores had to turn in a certain number of stamps each time they bought a steak or a bag of sugar. Other items not rationed were scarce: Silk stockings, hardware, and much else, were sometimes hard to find. Teenaged drivers found themselves unable to take the family car out for a casual trip. Trains and buses, in demand for troops traveling around the country, were often packed, with people standing in the aisles for hours. Clubs and restaurants were full: With a lot of products unavailable, especially automobiles—none of which were made in 1943 and 1944—people had money for entertainment.

Many, perhaps the majority of Americans, found themselves caught up in some sort of volunteer war work. Many served without pay on ration, draft, and other boards. Fearing air raids (although in fact none was attempted), cities were blacked out at night; thousands of people walked the streets of cities and towns at night as air-raid wardens, telling people to turn off lights or pull down blackout curtains. Other thousands acted as airplane spotters, reporting planes overhead to a central office. (There was far less air traffic then than there is today.) There was no everyday recycling of bottles, cans, and newspapers then; young children helped to collect these things and scrap metal, and rubber for reuse. Others started "Victory Gardens" in their backyards. The war touched nearly everybody. Boy and Girl Scout troops routinely worked on scrap drives, and drilled as aids to air-raid wardens and as messengers for local defense headquarters. People as young as twelve served as airplane spotters. Retired men and women became air-raid wardens. Countless hours were spent by Red Cross volunteers rolling bandages. Nearly everybody

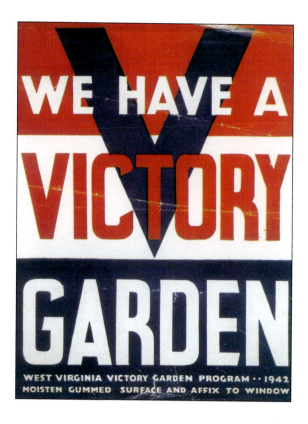

WEST VIRGINIA VICTORY GARDEN PROGRAM ·· 1942
MOISTEN GUMMED SURFACE AND AFFIX TO WINDOW

Americans dug up their backyards and baseball diamonds to plant what were known as Victory Gardens. Schoolchildren made themselves useful to the war effort by hoeing rows of corn and weeding beans.

did something for "the war effort."

Psychologically, one important effect of the war was the sense most people had that their lives were on hold. Young men and women put off marriage and children as the men went off to fight. Other men abandoned schools and colleges to join the army. Businessmen turned from the civilian products they had been making to guns and bullets. Youngsters in school gave up planning for the future, sure that they would first serve in the military. Many young wives and mothers struggled to make some kind of family life as they worried constantly about husbands fighting in distant places they had never heard of. The war was the primary fact of American life.

One group of Americans who perhaps felt this effect the most, aside from the men doing the actual fighting, were the thousands of Japanese and their children, most of them living on the West Coast. With the outbreak of the war with Japan, many Americans grew fearful of the Japanese among them, whom they suspected of treachery. The govern-

Americans were urged to buy government bonds to help pay for the war. With few civilian goods being manufactured, millions of Americans bought the bonds, giving many of them the first significant savings they had ever had.

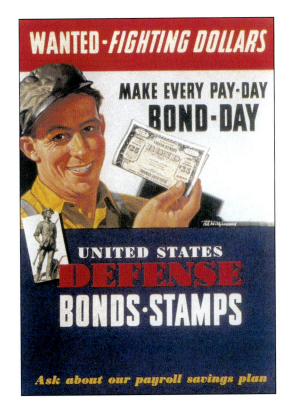

ment singled out about 2,000 as possible enemy agents, and arrested many of them. But with the initial Japanese victories in the Pacific, fears grew, and some people, both in and out of the government, demanded that the Japanese be interned in special camps for the duration of the war.

For the 40,000 Japanese who had been born in Japan and had not been permitted to take out citizenship, some excuse for internment might be made: They were not, after all, citizens. But for the 70,000 Japanese-Americans who had been born in the United States, and thus were American citizens, internment would be a clear violation of traditional rights. Some people saw this and objected, but the feeling against Japan, especially as the cruelties toward American prisoners of war became known, was strong, and in the spring of 1942 internment was begun of 112,000 Japanese, huge numbers of them American citizens. German-Americans and Italian-Americans were never interned in this way, and many historians have concluded that the internment of the Japanese was

Japanese Americans being checked into an internment camp. As many of these people were American citizens, the internment regulations were clearly unconstitutional, but the government enforced them anyway.

due to racial prejudice. Eventually, lawsuits were brought to the Supreme Court, which upheld some elements of discrimination against Japanese and their children, but ruled that those whose loyalty was not in doubt could not be detained. In fact, however, most of those interned were not released until the war was over.

But even though the war disrupted American lives, the fact is that for most of them World War II did a lot more good than it did harm. For one thing, it started the United States on a wave of prosperity that would last for almost thirty years, and which in some respects continued through the rest of the twentieth century. It helped to lower racial barriers and bring African-Americans closer to the mainstream. It threw together in the military service, in factories, in volunteer organizations, many people who might not ordinarily have met, and helped to create a more cohesive society. Compared with the suffering endured by the peoples of the other combatants, who saw their cities bombed, their farms shelled, and their children starved, World War II was, as has been said, for Americans at least, the last good war. It was, of course, the soldiers in the fighting who as always carried the burden. Those dead paid the debts of the living.

CHAPTER V

The War in the Pacific

The war in the Pacific is not as easy to understand as the war in Europe where most of the fighting took place on a single landmass between large armies in deadly combat. The arena of war in Asia was the entire Pacific Ocean, the thousands of islands that dotted it, and the lands that surrounded it. Many of the important battles were sea fights between great battleships and aircraft carriers, although of course in the end troops had to slog it out on the ground.

The Japanese never had any intention of invading the United States. Their idea was to take control of as much of Asia and the Pacific islands as they thought they required, especially the European colonies with the raw materials Japan desperately needed—oil, rubber, tin, and much else. They planned to make two thrusts southward from their home island. One would go into Southeast Asia through what are now Vietnam, Thailand, Myanmar, and Malaya and into Indonesia. The other would go through Taiwan and the Philippines and eventually meet with the first thrust in Indonesia. There would be smaller thrusts as well.

The Japanese estimated that it would take the United States a year and a half to recover from the attack on Pearl Harbor and subsequent attacks on the Philippines and other, smaller American island possessions in the Pacific. By that time Japan would have built strong military bases throughout the whole eastern half of the Pacific, and would be very difficult for the Americans to dislodge. Japan would then possess one of the world's greatest empires, and would finally have gained its place in the sun.

At first, things went extremely well for the Japanese. The native peoples in Thailand, the Philippines, and elsewhere had few forces of their

This unusual sketch was made by a Japanese artist and was meant to suggest how Japanese troops, carrying the flag in the rear, would drive out American defenders, in the foreground. The Japanese at first badly underestimated both American abilities and determination to win the war.

own. They depended upon the European colonizers to defend them. But the English, Dutch, French, and Belgian colonizers, at war with Germany, had few forces to spare for the Pacific. On Pearl Harbor morning the Japanese caught the Americans by surprise not only in Hawaii, but in the Philippines, too. There they destroyed the American air force on the ground, and soon after landed troops on the northern part of Luzon, one of the main Philippine islands. American and Filipino defenders fought and fell back again and again, until they were bottled up in the Bataan Peninsula at one end of Luzon. For weeks they held out, but finally in April with food running out, they were forced to surrender. The Japanese did not accept the idea of an honorable surrender: They believed a soldier must fight until he dies. Thus they were contemptuous of the American prisoners and treated them brutally. During the march to the prison camp they jabbed them with bayonets, cut some heads off, whipped and beat them. When news of the sixty-five-mile Bataan Death March, as it came to be called, became known, Americans decided to show the Japanese no mercy when their turn came. And they did not.

In the Pacific war, much of the strategy had to do with controlling this or that little island which could be used for storing supplies, resting troops, or mounting attacks on enemy shipping. A lot of heavy and costly fighting raged over tiny islands with only temporary military value. Though few Americans had ever even heard of them, control of the seas would depend on who controlled these islands. Japanese and American navies would play critical roles, and during the first months after Pearl Harbor they fought several great naval battles.

With their easy initial successes, the Japanese grew overconfident. They decided to take bases closer to the United States, including ones in the Aleutian Islands near Alaska (two of which the Japanese briefly held), and Midway Island in the middle of the Pacific west of the Hawaiian Islands. They sent a huge fleet steaming into the Pacific. The American fleet, under Admiral Chester Nimitz, knew they were coming. He caught

During the Death March from Bataan, soldiers who were wounded or exhausted were often carried by friends. Japanese were scornful of men who surrendered, and killed many of the sick or wounded along the way.

the Japanese by surprise northwest of Midway. American dive-bombers from aircraft carriers and from Midway Island hit the Japanese carriers while their planes were refueling on deck. The dive-bombers laid their bombs among the planes, throwing flaming gasoline everywhere. Within minutes three big Japanese carriers were in flames. Although the Americans lost some ships in the Battle of Midway, the Japanese lost far more. It was a great victory for the Americans and it showed that aircraft carriers would be the indispensable weapon in the naval war.

But it required immense bravery on the part of naval pilots. In the Battle of the Coral Sea, not long before the Battle of Midway, a navy pilot, John Powers, decided to dive down below 1,000 feet before he released his bomb, to make sure it hit its target. One of his bombs helped to sink the Japanese carrier *Shoho* in the Coral Sea. The next day, as they

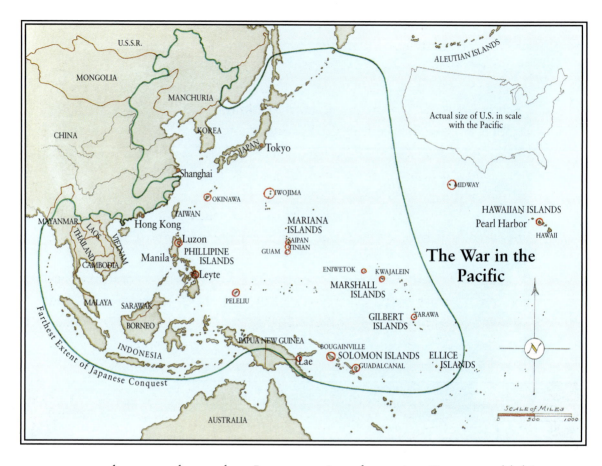

The War in the Pacific

prepared to attack another Japanese aircraft carrier, Powers told his friends, "I'm going to get a hit if I have to lay it on their flight deck." He dived through antiaircraft fire and Japanese planes and got a direct hit, but he had gone so close that the blast from his own bomb destroyed him and his plane. Powers was posthumously awarded the Congressional Medal of Honor.

By the middle of 1942 the Americans were no longer on the defensive in the Pacific, but were ready to attack. (It should be remembered that the Pacific fighting included the British, Australians, and others, but the main burden was carried by the Americans.) The Americans realized that

Australia was a natural home base for them in the Pacific, where they could store supplies, train men, and bring in ships for repairs. The Japanese knew this, too, and hoped to establish strongholds on nearby islands in order to threaten Allied shipping going in and out of Australia. They built bases in a group called the Solomon Islands. The Americans decided to drive them out of the Solomons and invaded one of the group, called Guadalcanal. The fight for Guadalcanal typified the jungle warfare that the Pacific war entailed. Not only did soldiers have a deadly enemy to deal with, but they were constantly beset by fierce heat, torrential rains, tropical diseases, and stinging insects. In such conditions a soldier's life could be awfully miserable even when there was no fighting to be done.

The battle for Guadalcanal seesawed back and forth. There were several naval battles in the waters around the islands, as the Americans and Japanese fought to keep the other side from bringing in supplies and reinforcements. Each side won some of these engagements and lost some.

A combat artist's painting of the action on Guadalcanal. Fighting in the hot, fetid jungle was exhausting.

Combat artist Tom Lea, later a well-known illustrator, painted this picture of soldiers on Peleiu, one of the dozens of little-known islands that the U.S. military had to take from the Japanese one at a time.

During one fight coastguardsman Douglas Munro, in charge of a landing craft, was ordered to bring off 500 Marines trapped ashore by the Japanese. He went in alone with his own boat to investigate the situation, braving Japanese machine-gun fire, and brought out thirty wounded Marines. He then went back to the beach leading two other boats. Using his own boat as a shield, he fired on the Japanese with his own machine gun until the rescue boats had got clear. He was fatally hit, and as he died said, "Did we get them all off?" He was the only coastguardsman to be awarded a Congressional Medal of Honor in the war.

By mid-November 1942, the Americans had finally managed to establish naval dominance around Guadalcanal. Japanese supplies were cut off. American reinforcements poured in, and in February 1943, the Japanese gave up, and pulled out what remained of their half-starved troops. It had been an American victory, but it had not been an easy one, and American troops, fighting in the jungle, had suffered intensely for it.

Through 1943 and into 1944 the Americans and their allies, mostly Australians, pressed along the island of New Guinea towards the Philippines. On the way they fought a bloody battle to take the tiny atoll of Tarawa in the Gilbert Islands. All but 17 of the 4,600 Japanese soldiers chose to die rather than surrender. Of the 5,000 Marines who landed in the initial assault, 1,500 were dead or wounded on the first day. Tarawa taught Americans some hard-earned lessons about amphibious

Making landings on Pacific Island beaches was deadly work, with very high losses during the initial assault. Men charged the beaches knowing they had a good chance of dying in the attack. The army rarely released pictures of American dead, but this photograph of the beach on the island of Tarawa got through.

landings: They were going to be costly in the lives of men. However, Tarawa showed that they could be successful.

Through 1944 the Americans continued their "island-hopping," taking one small dot of land after the next. In most cases the Japanese troops chose to die rather than surrender, usually in a last, desperate suicide attack. This refusal to give up, even when the fight was lost, would have important consequences in American thinking later on.

By this time, too, the American fleet was gaining the upper hand over the Japanese fleet. The great American industrial machine was turning out ships faster than the Japanese could. The light Japanese Zero fighter planes were no match for the heavy American navy Hellcats. During the Battle of the Philippine Sea, known as "the Marianas Turkey Shoot," so much of the Japanese fleet was damaged that "Japanese carrier strength was a thing of the past," as one historian has put it.

It was now time for a return to the Philippines. The landing was planned for the island of Leyte, through the Leyte Gulf. The Japanese fleet, as badly wounded as it was, was not dead. Its admirals decided to gather the remains of their forces, which would be larger than the American fleet supporting the landing, and blow the Americans out of the water. The naval Battle of Leyte Gulf was a confused fight, fought in six separate actions by three huge forces of Japanese ships against the Americans. But without an effective force of carrier planes, the Japanese were badly handicapped. American bombers and torpedo planes could attack Japanese ships at will. Fighting over hundreds of miles of sea, the Americans gained an amazing victory. The Japanese lost three battleships, four carriers, and nineteen other ships—300,000 tons of ships opposed to 37,000 tons lost by the Americans. In terms of ships involved, the Battle of Leyte Gulf was the greatest naval battle of *all time*. In its waning moments, the desperate Japanese unveiled a new weapon—the suicide plane. The *kamikaze* pilots were given special belts into which a thousand Japanese women had each woven a single stitch, and went

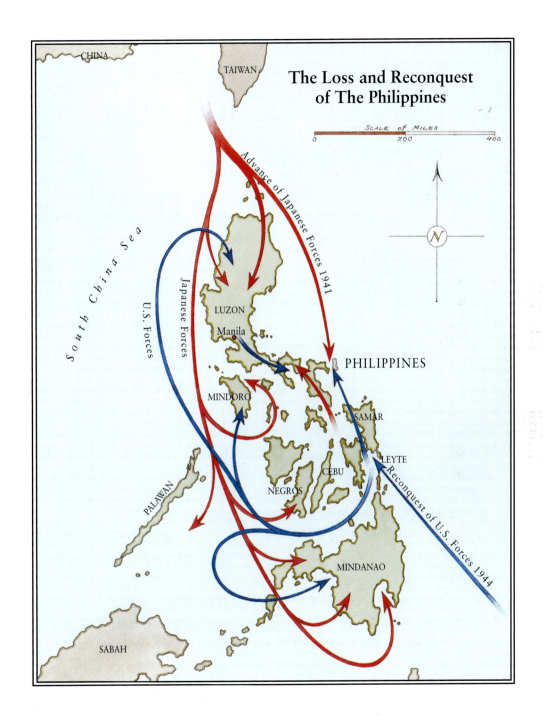

The Loss and Reconquest of The Philippines

Suicide planes were very difficult to stop. Coming in as fast as they did, gunners had difficulty training their antiaircraft weapons on them quickly enough. However, in this picture made in the Marianas, navy gunners knocked the suicide plane down in time.

through an elaborate ritual before taking off. Kamikazes, diving to their deaths, were difficult for naval gunners to fend off, but they turned out to be less effective than the Japanese had hoped.

After Leyte Gulf, the Japanese fleet was a ruin, although still capable of occasional actions. American landings in the Philippines were successful, but as ever, the fight to take the islands was long and costly: 14,000 Americans died there. But by the beginning of 1945 it was clear that the Japanese, now without an effective navy or air force, were doomed. They should have given up the fight, but that was not the way they were thinking. Premier Tojo resigned as a consequence of the heavy losses at Leyte Gulf. The new government decided to use kamikaze planes flying from Japan—without enough fuel to return—to destroy the American fleet, and then fight desperately in the Japanese islands, themselves, hoping that the Americans would tire of the fight, and negotiate a peace. The Allies, however, had already announced that they would only accept an "unconditional surrender" from the Axis nations. The Americans would fight on in the Pacific.

Indeed, the Americans, freed after May 1945 from the fighting in Europe, were already bringing the war home to the Japanese. They now had islands close enough to Japan to bomb Japanese cities. However, the

But often the suicide planes got through. The U.S.S. Bunker Hill *took hits from two kamikaze planes within minutes. 396 men were killed, and the ship was badly damaged, but survived.*

flight was too long for protective escort fighters to fly along with the bombers. The Americans needed bases closer to Japan, and it was decided to take Iwo Jima, a tiny volcanic island six hundred miles from Japan. The fight for Iwo Jima was brutal. In the first wave, American Marines sank up to their boot tops in volcanic ash. At the southern end of the island the Japanese had dug deeply into Mount Suribachi. They had to be killed in their dugouts one by one by flame throwers, grenades, and explosive satchel charges. The Americans had figured they could take the island in five days; it took over a month and cost 21,000 Japanese dead, 6,800 Americans killed and another 18,000 wounded. It was one of the bloodiest battles of the Pacific war. It has remained memorable on that account, but also because of the famous picture of Marines raising the flag on Mount Suribachi, which has been printed many thousands of times, and cast as a statue in many places.

Next, the Americans attacked the island of Okinawa, larger than Iwo Jima and even closer to Japan. Here again the Japanese, dug deeply into cliffs and ridges at the southern end of the island, let the Americans land uncontested, and forced the attackers to drive them out of the rocky cliffs one at a time. Most preferred to die rather than surrender. To escape the dreaded American flame throwers, the Japanese often took poison or retreated to the backs of caves and blew themselves up with hand grenades. Once more the carnage was horrifying: When the battle was over in June, only 7,000 of 77,000 Japanese soldiers were alive. Another 100,000 Okinawan civilians had died. Over 12,000 Americans had also died.

Back home, in the fall of 1944, President Roosevelt had run for an unprecedented fourth term. So popular was he that he easily won, along with his vice president, former senator from Missouri, Harry S. Truman. Franklin D. Roosevelt was now old and tired from battling first the Great Depression, and then the war. While the fighting was on in Okinawa he died, and Harry Truman became president. Roosevelt is today considered one of America's greatest presidents, and a great war leader.

Unfortunately, he had not confided much in Truman. One of the things the new president discovered was that for several years scientists in America had been working on a devastating new weapon, the most powerful the world had ever seen. Back in 1939, the mathematical genius Albert Einstein had written Roosevelt, saying that an immensely powerful bomb could be created by splitting the atom. Roosevelt had authorized the building of such a bomb. At his death the atomic bomb was almost ready, and on July 16, 1945, it was tested at Alamagordo, New Mexico. The explosion was so powerful it left even the scientists who had designed it awestruck.

In high government circles, there was not much debate about using the bomb by the few who knew the secret. Roosevelt, Truman, and their advisors had all assumed that the atomic bomb was not merely to be a threat, but was to be actually dropped on the enemy. As the final moments arrived, some people suggested that it be demonstrated to the Japanese in some unoccupied area. However, the general opinion was that if the demonstration worked, the Japanese would believe it was a trick, and if it didn't work, it would become all the harder to get the Japanese to take it seriously. Nonetheless, President Truman knew that a few Japanese leaders were trying to find a way out of the war, and to support them he warned that the United States possessed new and terrible weapons, without spelling out what they were. But the Japanese leaders appeared determined to fight to their deaths. American troops faced the prospect of much more deadly island-hopping and then an invasion of the main Japanese islands themselves.

On August 6, 1945, an American bomber, the *Enola Gay*, named for the pilot's mother, dropped an atomic bomb on the Japanese city of Hiroshima. Probably 80,000 people died immediately (there is some debate about the exact figure), tens of thousands more would die lingering deaths, and the city was destroyed. On August 8, Russia hastily entered the war against Japan and invaded Manchuria, the area Japan

Yet one more oft-printed picture to come out of the war shows the famous "mushroom cloud" rising above Hiroshima after the first atomic bomb was dropped.

had taken from China at the very beginning of hostilities. Still the Japanese did not ask for peace, and on August 9 the Americans dropped another atomic bomb, this time on Nagasaki, destroying that city and killing tens of thousands more Japanese. The next day Japan offered to surrender, on condition that the emperor, sacred to the Japanese, would remain on his throne and not be harmed. Although the Allies had originally insisted on unconditional surrender, they were willing to accept this one condition in order to save the hundreds of thousands of lives that would have been lost in an invasion of Japan. Agreements were completed by August 15, 1945—known since as V-J Day. Finally World War II was over.

There has always been much argument over the morality of America's use of the atomic bomb. Many people believe that such a terrible weapon should never have been used against civilians, especially women and children. We must be careful, in looking at this question, of the danger of what historians call "presentism," that is, looking at past events with the attitudes and beliefs of the present. We must try to view the past with the attitudes and perspectives of those days.

For one thing, at the time, most Americans were angry, indeed enraged, at the Japanese for the surprise attack on Pearl Harbor, the Bataan Death March with its beheadings and other atrocities, the ill-treatment of prisoners. For a second, while all the belligerent nations eventually engaged in the mass bombing of civilians, the Japanese had been first in their attack on Shanghai in 1937. In 1945 Americans, rightly or wrongly, felt no pity for the Japanese.

For another, the *kamikaze* planes, and the suicide charges had convinced many people, including government and military officials, that an attack on the Japanese mainland would be bloody—look at the death toll on Iwo Jima and Okinawa. Not only would perhaps a hundred thousand Americans die, but hundreds of thousands—perhaps even millions—of Japanese would be killed by an American invasion of Japan, with the inevitable shelling and bombing of cities. The fight on Okinawa had, after all, killed 100,000 hapless citizens. It is almost certainly true that more Japanese would have died in an invasion than did so from both atomic bombs. Ironically, thus, the atomic bombs probably *saved* many Japanese lives. The argument is sometimes made that the Japanese were about to surrender anyway; that Truman knew this and had the bombs dropped as a way of scaring the Communist Soviet Union into peaceful post-war behavior. Not many historians accept this.

Another question that comes up is this: Is it more immoral to kill masses of civilians in a war with a single bomb than with a thousand? The mass bombing of Shanghai by the Japanese, the German bombing of Warsaw, and the Allied bombing of Dresden had each killed tens of thousands of people in the course of a few days. Indeed, an American raid on Tokyo five months before the atomic attack, using ordinary bombs, had killed as many people as the atomic bomb had at Hiroshima.

Finally, suppose President Truman had not used the atomic bomb in order to spare Japanese civilians, and instead had ordered a bloody invasion of the Japanese mainland. Suppose, after 100,000 American men had died in the invasion, it came out that Truman could have saved those lives by using the atomic bomb to kill Japanese instead. He would certainly have been driven from office, possibly impeached, perhaps even tried as a traitor to his country. There was simply no possibility, in 1945, that any American president could have refused to use the bomb. Once it existed, it would be used. There never has been anything very moral about war.

CHAPTER VI

Summing Up

World War II was one of the great events in human history, surely the central event of the twentieth century. It quite simply changed the world. It left formerly great nations like England, Germany, and France weakened, their colonies stripped away. As a result of the war, within a decade hundreds of millions of people found themselves living under vastly different governments from the ones they had begun the war under—Czechs, Poles, Hungarians, Estonians, and others, controlled by the Russians; former colonials like Indians and Malayans ruled by their own leaders; the Chinese under a dictatorship rather than an at least outwardly democratic government. The United States, before the war one of several major powers, was, at its close, the dominant nation, challenged only by the Union of Soviet Socialist Republics, that is Russia and fifteen smaller states all controlled from Moscow.

Despite the chaos, death, and destruction, the war did much long-term good. For one thing, it stopped the march of the fascist dictators, with their cruel policies of enslavement and genocide, from dominating much, if not all, of the world. Perhaps more important, the triumph of the United States in particular helped to spread democratic ideas. The struggle for democracy has been long and hard, and is still far from won; but it is clear that, however slowly, the world is becoming more democratic. And for the United States, it brought the end of the grinding poverty of the Great Depression, and helped to push the nation into an unprecedented fifty years of the greatest prosperity any nation has ever enjoyed.

But the costs were heavy. It was the combat soldiers who paid the greatest price. Unfortunately for them, generals invariably prefer experienced troops, however emotionally exhausted, to green troops, however

The destruction caused by World War II is difficult for us to imagine today. The battle for Monte Cassino, just one of the countless battles, destroyed this famous monastery. Similar scenes could be seen in thousands of places around the world at the war's end.

fresh. The same regiments, divisions, armies were again and again thrown into battle. These soldiers knew that if they weren't killed or wounded this day, this week, this month, they probably would be the next. In truth, a very small number of people did the actual fighting. Sixteen million Americans served in the armed forces during World War II. Not more than about 10 percent of them saw combat. Of these about 1.5 million men, some 400,000 were killed, another half a million were wounded—meaning that if you were in combat for any length of time, chances were much better than 50-50 that you were going to get hit sooner or later.

Many soldiers grew bitter: Why were they facing death again and again when other Americans exactly like them were safely behind the lines loading ships or typing reports, or working for good money in factories thousands of miles away? There was a divide between those who had been in combat, and those who had not. Even experienced veterans found it difficult to explain to friends and family what combat was really like—the shock of it, the emotional exhaustion it could produce, the steady, deep fear. For most people, death is a tragedy that comes into their lives only occasionally, and then one by one. The soldier in combat daily sees on the beach, the field, the mountainside, dozens, even hundreds, of bodies of people like himself, many with their flesh ripped open, heads smashed, limbs gone, flies buzzing around their wounds. The sight is often incomprehensible.

But what Americans suffered was minor compared with the losses of other nations. Two million Japanese died, and somewhere between twenty and thirty million Russians. The British, Germans, Italians, and others also took heavy losses, not only to soldiers and civilians, but to cities and towns that were the scenes of the fighting. The good that came out of World War II came at a heavy cost.

And it is clear now that it need not have happened. Part of the problem was the feeling of the Germans and Japanese, in particular, that they

But some good did come out of the war. Aside from ridding the world of several dictators, it produced many major technological advances that have done much for humanity. New drugs developed during the war have saved millions of lives. Penicillin was discovered before the war, but was only mass-produced during the war. Here penicillin is being processed.

deserved to be higher up in the pecking order of nations than they believed they were. They wanted some glory, and they were willing to follow leaders who promised it to them. Part of the problem was the personality of Adolf Hitler, who believed that he was the infallible leader sent to bring the Germans back to greatness. Part of the problem was the willingness of various groups in Germany to support Hitler, because they believed he was serving their ends—particularly by strengthening the military and drawing a line against communism.

But the fault lay not just with the Axis nations. The Allies, including the United States, refused to see what the dictators intended to do until it was too late. Franklin Roosevelt saw it, and so did Winston Churchill; but they could not gather public opinion behind them until the shooting started and the blood began to flow. In the end, in democracies the people decide; and to decide rightly they have to take the trouble to keep themselves informed about the world around them.

Hitler and Pearl Harbor taught Americans that the world could be a dangerous place. They promised themselves they would not let dictators run rampant again. This determination would underlie the United States' defense and foreign policy for at least the rest of the twentieth century. (For the unfolding of America's postwar foreign policy, see the volume in this series called *United States in the Cold War*.)

BIBLIOGRAPHY

For Students

Black, Wallace B. and Jean F. Blashfield. World War II battles series. Sixteen short volumes include *America Prepares for War* and *The War Behind the Lines*. New York: Crestwood House, 1992.

Cannon, Marian G. *Dwight David Eisenhower: War Hero and President*. New York: Franklin Watts, 1990.

Dunnahoo, Terry. *Pearl Harbor: America Enters the War*. New York: Franklin Watts, 1991.

Freedman, Russell. *Franklin Delano Roosevelt*. New York: Clarion, 1990.

Leavell, J. Perry. *Harry S. Truman*. New York: Chelsea House, 1988.

Levine, Ellen. *A Fence Away from Freedom: Japanese Americans and World War II*. New York: Putnam, 1995.

Lubetkin, Wendy. *George Marshall*. New York: Chelsea House, 1989.

Marrin, Albert. *The Airman's War: World War II in the Sky*. New York: Atheneum, 1982.

Pietrusza, David. *The Invasion of Normandy*. San Diego, CA: Lucent, 1995.

Rice, Earl. *The Battle of Midway*. San Diego, CA: Lucent, 1995.

Takaki, Ronald. *Hiroshima: Why America Dropped the Atomic Bomb*. Boston: Little, Brown, 1995.

Young, Robert. *Hiroshima: Fifty Years of Debate*. New York: DillonPress, 1994.

Zeinert, Karen. *Those Incredible Women of World War II*. Brookfield, CT: Millbrook Press, 1996.

For Teachers

Ambrose, Stephen E. *Eisenhower*. 2 vols. New York: Simon & Schuster, 1983 and 1984.

Bell, Philip M. H. *The Origins of the Second World War in Europe*. 2nd ed. New York: Longman, 1997.

Beschloss, Michael. *Eisenhower: A Centennial Life*. New York: Harper Collins, 1990.

Blum, John Morton. *V Was for Victory: Politics and American Culture During World War II*. New York: Harcourt Brace Jovanovich, 1976.

Feis, Herbert. *The Atom Bomb and the End of World War II*. Princeton: Princeton University Press, 1966.

Gilbert, Martin. *The Second World War*. Rev. ed. New York: Henry Holtand Company, 1991.

Goodwin, Doris Kearns. *No Ordinary Time, Franklin and Eleanor Roosevelt: The Homefront in World War II*. New York, Simon & Schuster, 1994.

Iriye, Akira. *Origins of the Second World War in Asia and the Pacific*. New York: Longman, 1987.

Keegan, John. *The Second World War*. New York: Penguin Books, 1990.

Kennedy, David M. *Freedom From Fear: The American People in Depression and War, 1929–1945*. New York: Oxford University Press, 1999.

Linderman, Gerald F. *The World Within War: America's Combat Experience in World War II*. New York: The Free Press, 1997.

Lingeman, Richard. *Don't You Know There's a War On?* New York, Putnam, 1970.

Prange, Gordon W. *At Dawn We Slept: The Untold Story of Pearl Harbor*. New York: McGraw Hill, 1981.

Utley, Jonathan G. *Going to War with Japan, 1937–1941*. Knoxville: University of Tennessee Press, 1985.

Winkler, Allan M. *Homefront USA: America During World War II*. 2nd ed. Arlington Heights, IL: H. Davidson, 2000.

Page numbers for illustrations are in **boldface**

JAMES LINCOLN COLLIER is the author of a number of books both for adults and for young people, including the social history *The Rise of Selfishness in America*. He is also noted for his biographies and historical studies in the field of jazz. Together with his brother, Christopher Collier, he has written a series of award-winning historical novels for children widely used in schools, including the Newbery Honor classic, *My Brother Sam Is Dead*. A graduate of Hamilton College, he lives with his wife in New York City.

CHRISTOPHER COLLIER grew up in Fairfield County, Connecticut and attended public schools there. He graduated from Clark University in Worcester, Massachusetts and earned M.A. and Ph.D. degrees at Columbia University in New York City. After service in the Army and teaching in secondary schools for several years, Mr. Collier began teaching college in 1961. He is now Professor of History at the University of Connecticut and Connecticut State Historian. Mr. Collier has published many scholarly and popular books and articles about Connecticut and American history. With his brother, James, he is the author of nine historical novels for young adults, the best known of which is *My Brother Sam Is Dead*. He lives with his wife Bonnie, a librarian, in Orange, Connecticut.